This book is about
Hunters and farmers of prehistory

WHAT IS PREHISTORY?
Prehistory is the name archaeologists use for an enormous period of time in the past when there are no written records. In Britain that is before the coming of the Romans. Today we have lots of different ways of recording what happens. One way is to publish newspapers – can you think of three others?

1. Newspapers 2. ....
3. .... 4. ....

WHAT DO ARCHAEOLOGISTS DO?
Archaeologists are those people who investigate the remains of the past. They search out, record and try to understand the *evidence* for the past. In this book you will discover lots of things about the prehistoric peoples which can be pieced together from the evidence which remains.

Look at the sand-timer. You may have used one to time a 3-minute egg. This sand-timer shows the enormous number of years that make up part of prehistory – from the end of the ice age. Compare that with the tip which represents the Roman period up to the present day.

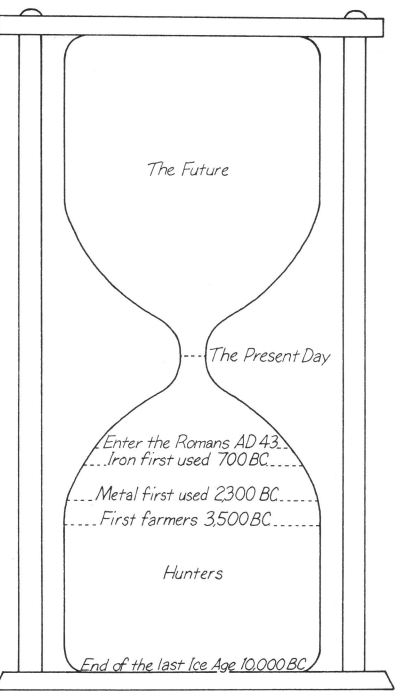

Why not try making a sand-timer for your family? Find out as much as you can about your family in the past by asking your relatives and fill in the dates below.

Name................
Date of birth......

A NOTE ABOUT DATES
Up to the birth of Christ you count backwards from 0 and put BC (before Christ) after the date. After that we use AD which stands for *Anno Domini* which is Latin for 'in the year of the Lord'.

Be an archaeological detective

Archaeologists are really detectives hunting out the clues which help them find out what happened in the past. Think about what police detectives search for when they investigate a crime like a robbery.

POLICE DETECTIVES are on the look out for	ARCHAEOLOGICAL DETECTIVES are on the look out for
▽	▽
EVIDENCE which might be	EVIDENCE which might be
▽	▽
fingerprints/room in disorder/broken window/ forced desk/list of objects stolen from owner/talks with neighbours	broken pottery/animal bones/ seeds/remains of houses/ tools/remains of burial or 'sacred' sites

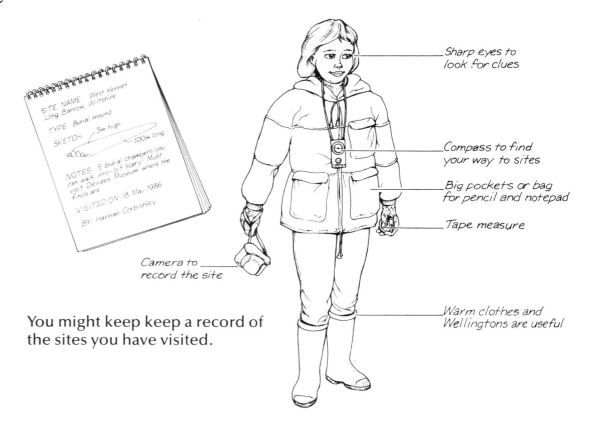

You might keep keep a record of the sites you have visited.

SURVIVAL OF THE EVIDENCE

Often many of the clues which would have helped piece together the story have rotted away or been re-used for something else in later times. Imagine what it would be like for police detectives to hunt for their clues 2000 years after the robbery! That is exactly what archaeologists have to do.

FINGERPRINTS OF THE PAST

Look for the archaeological evidence in the rest of this book and imagine piecing together the story of the past from just a few clues.

Imagine the girl here buried in the ground for 2000 years. Write down which parts of both her body and what she is wearing and carrying would survive best. Suggestions on page 16.

SURVIVES BEST   SURVIVES WORST

...and discover some sites

JOIN THE DOTS TO MAKE A MAP

This map (guess where?) shows a number of important prehistoric sites which you might like to visit. There are a great many more which you can search out using the recommended books on page 16 and by asking at your local museum or library. Good time-hunting!

BEWARE!

Archaeological sites are an endangered species. Once we destroy the last burial mound, for example, we can't grow any more! Please do not dig into sites or use a metal detector. Help to protect our past by looking out for it.

WHAT THE SYMBOLS MEAN

- Caves where hunters once lived (pages 4-5)
- Flint Mines (page 6)
- Burial Mounds (page 7)
- Henges and Stone Circles (pages 8-9)
- Hill Forts and Settlements (page 14)

SCOTLAND

There are lots of prehistoric sites to be discovered in Scotland. Look out for the great stones at Callanish and the remarkable village at Skara Brae on the Orkneys.

Hunters, fishers and gatherers

There have been human beings on earth for at least the last 2½ million years. People first came to Britain about 300,000 years ago when it was actually joined to the mainland of Europe. We call these people hunter-gatherers. It was the period of the last ice age. At the coldest times it was impossible to live in Britain and the hunters must have moved south. At other times trees and plants grew and there were animals such as mammoths, woolly rhinoceros, horses, giant deer, reindeer, wolves, foxes and bear to hunt.

It is very difficult to find evidence of these early hunters. We know that in the warmer periods the hunters lived in the open and that when the weather became worse they moved into caves. Here it is easier for archaeologists to find evidence – bone of animals, broken flint tools and the remains of fires, for example. Because a number of tools and weapons were made of flints or other types of stone, archaeologists call this period of prehistory the stone age.

I spotted flint tools of the earliest hunters in Britain at ....
I visited the cave site of ....

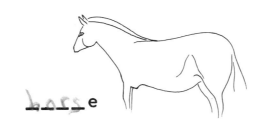
h o r s e

R e i n d e e r

_ _ s _ _

CAVE ARTISTS

During the period from about 30,000 to 8,000 BC the hunters in western Europe made paintings and engravings on the walls of caves, and engravings on bone and sculpture. The finest examples of the hunters' art are in France and Spain although a few carvings on bone have been found in Britain.

_ h _ _ _ _ _ _ _

Which of these animals exist today and where?

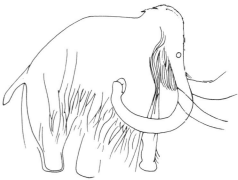
M _ _ _ _ _ h

MAKE YOUR OWN CAVE PAINTING

The artists often had bumpy cave walls to paint on. You could make your own very simply: tear a piece from a cardboard box. Scrumple it up then roughly flatten it out. You will have a rough, bumpy surface to draw and paint on.

What to paint with? Try
★ your fingers
★ a stick
★ a stick with one end soaked and mashed so that it is like a rough brush
★ making a brush with hair tied on to a stick (next time you have your hair cut save some!)

The hunters' colours: yellow, red, orange, brown and black are the most common.

What to paint: any of the animals drawn or written about on this page. The hunter-artists often painted groups of animals.

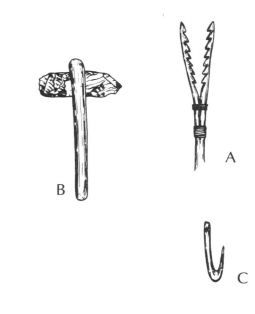

What did the hunters use these tools for?

Answers

A. For spearing fish   B. An axe for chopping trees   C. Fish hook made of bone

A PICTURE TO COLOUR IN

A hunter-gatherers' camp based on evidence found at the site of Star Carr in North Yorkshire, dated to about 7,500 BC. Notice how the people are using all the parts of the animal – flesh, bone and skin. Wood is used for shelter, fire, handles for tools, a dugout canoe and platforms over the marshy ground on the edge of the lake.

On the back cover you will see the game 'Hunting the elk'. At the end of the last ice age the ice melted, and Britain became an island between 6000 and 5000 BC. The whole countryside changed and great forests grew – first pine trees then hazel, oak, elm and lime. The people still hunted, fished and gathered food but the animals were smaller – no longer mammoth but elk, then deer, wild boar, fox, hare, wild cat and beaver.

First farmers in Britain

On the last page you saw the hunter-gatherers of Britain after the last ice age. Did you notice the dog? This was probably the first attempt to 'domesticate' an animal. However these people were not farmers.

The first farmers of Britain came from Europe around 3500 BC. They brought with them animals for breeding – cattle, sheep and goats and seeds of crops. There were two types of wheat, called Emmer and Einkorn, barley and flax (see page 10).

These farmers made great changes to the landscape by clearing forests and by building farms and villages. In some parts of Britain their houses, constructed of wood, have not survived above ground. Here archaeologists have to excavate for evidence. In other places, such as at Skara Brae on mainland Orkney off the north coast of Scotland, parts of their stone houses do survive.

These early farmers needed flint (or other stone) to make tools. They found large supplies of it in various parts of Britain – for example, the hard stone found in North Wales and Cumbria was ideal for making axes. In Sussex and in East Anglia mines were dug to take out 'seams' of flint.

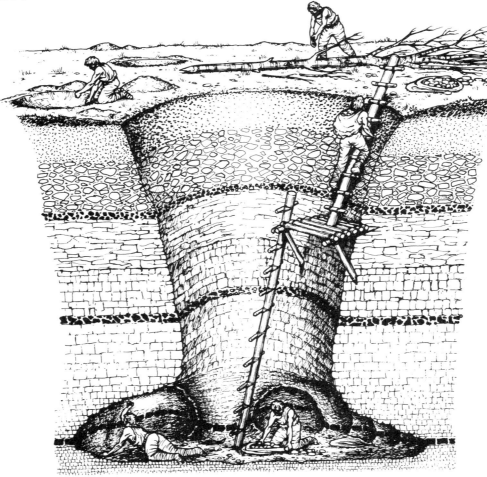

GRIMES GRAVES
This was an 'open-cast' mine in Norfolk which operated from 2100 BC to about 1600 BC. Open-cast means open holes in the ground. The miners dug away the sandy soil with shovels made from the shoulder blades of oxen but did most of the digging with picks made from the antlers cast off by red deer. The flint was used to make arrow and spear heads to hunt with (and perhaps to fight, too), scrapers to clear animal skins, knives to cut up the flesh and axes to cut down trees.

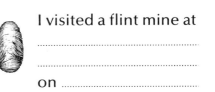

I visited a flint mine at ....

on ....

Where should these tools go in the picture? (answer on page 16).

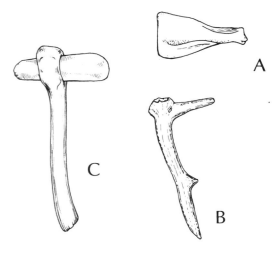

A

B

C

NOTE: Do you remember that archaeologists first called the hunting period the stone age? They also called the first farming period the stone age – but the new stone age. They were still finding flint or stone tools because they did not easily rot away *and* because people were not using metal yet. Bronze isn't discovered until page 9!

How they buried their dead

The farmers from Europe built huge stone structures of earth, wood and stone. Some were meeting places – we call them 'causeway camps' – where fairs, ceremonies and markets could be held. They also built burial mounds like the one below.

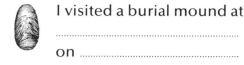

I visited a burial mound at ....
on ....

This one is a long barrow – about 100 metres in length and 3 metres high – built around 2500BC at West Kennet in Wiltshire. Imagine how many people were needed to dig the earth and drag the huge stones. It was used for over a thousand years to bury about 50 people. The drawing shows the burial rooms of stone where the bodies were put. All the bones were mixed up so archaeologists think that the bodies were left to rot away before burial. With the bodies were placed pottery and arrows. Notice how the entrance to the long mound is sealed by great stone blocks. Don't you think all these clues point to a people who had some beliefs, or ideas, about what happened after death?

WHAT DO YOU WANT BURIED WITH YOU?
Imagine you are writing your will – that's the orders you want carried out after your death. List, or draw, in this box what you would like to be buried with. You might choose the things you like best or objects which will show the archaeologists of the future what sort of person you are, or rather were!

Building Stonehenge

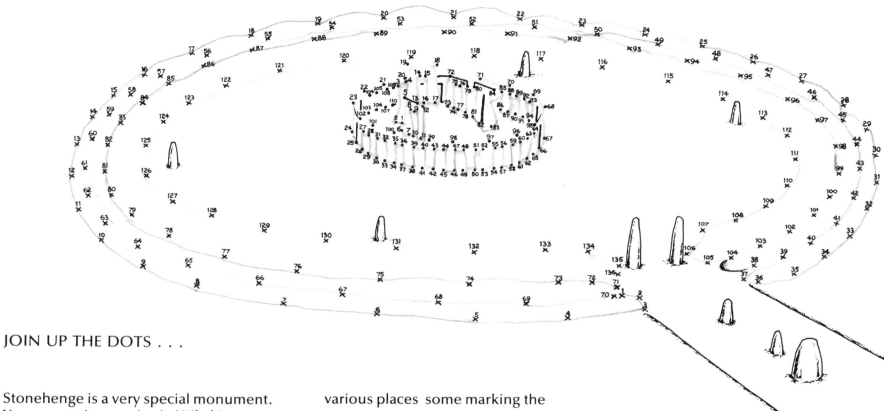

JOIN UP THE DOTS . . .

Stonehenge is a very special monument. You can see its remains in Wiltshire on Salisbury Plain. If you join up the dots and crosses you will see what it was like. To rediscover Stonehenge you will need two *different* colour pencils or felt tips.

FIRST use one colour to follow the symbols $x^1 \, x^2$ etc. This is what the site looked like when it was first built sometime between 3100 and 2100BC. It had a circular ditch and bank with a circle of holes just inside. Also there were stones standing upright in various places some marking the entrance.

THEN use another colour to follow the symbols $\bullet^1 \, \bullet^2$ etc. From about 2100BC onwards the site was changed several times. A stone circle was begun in the centre but never finished. If you join up the dots you will see how it looked in about 2000BC. Huge stones formed an inner circle and horseshoe shape. Later on it was changed again and by about 1500BC had a variety of stone circles and holes inside the original bank and ditch.

THE STONES

Two types of stones were used at Stonehenge. *Bluestones* were transported all the way from south-west Wales to form the original unfinished circle. Each bluestone weighed about 2 tonnes. The other type, called *sarsens*, came from the Marlborough Downs about 20 miles away. They formed the circle and horseshoe marked by dots here. The biggest weighed 50 tonnes each!

Using metal

From about 2300 BC the farming peoples in Britain began to use metal for their tools, weapons and jewellery. At first they used copper and gold. Then tin was discovered and by melting it with copper they got a much harder metal – bronze. Because of this discovery this period of prehistory is often called the bronze age.

During the 1600 years when these people used bronze they made a variety of different things.

One is called the palstave axe.

Making pottery

This type of bowl was used by the peple who first built henges.

This is a beaker found in West Kennet burial mound. It was put there with a burial during the early part of the bronze age.

In the period when people were using bronze, *urns* were often specially made to hold the cremated ashes of the dead. These were buried, with other objects, in round burial mounds.

Sometimes beakers had handles on like this one.

The early farmers of Britain used pottery for a number of their everyday objects – especially those for storing and cooking food.

POT DECORATION
Pots were decorated with a variety of things pressed into the wet clay –

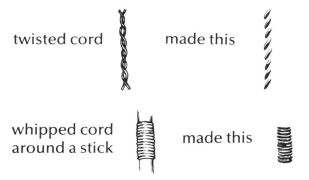

twisted cord ... made this

whipped cord around a stick ... made this

or you could make lines, notches, grooves and dots with sharp sticks, little bones (perhaps from birds) or combs. Why not try all these on your own pot.

MAKE YOUR OWN POT
You could easily make your own pot out of plasticine. Prehistoric potters made theirs by coiling long thin sausages of clay around to make the shape and then moulding it afterwards.

Draw and decorate your own pot on a separate sheet of paper

People of the iron age

CROPS

Here are some of the crops growing in the fields around Celtic settlements. They also ate a number of plants, like Fat Hen, which we would call weeds today.

EMMER WHEAT – on a Celtic coin

SPELT WHEAT – Cereals for bread, porridge or in stews

CELTIC BEAN – as a vegetable

FLAX For making linen cloth from stalks, leaves for animals to eat and oil from the seeds

There's a Celtic recipe for you to try on page 16.

From about 700 BC the farming peoples in Britain started to use iron as well as bronze. This period, up to the Roman invasion of AD 43, is usually called the iron age. The people were called Celts. Many of them (see page 12) could afford richly-decorated objects. They lived on small farms, or in farming settlements of just a few houses or in hill forts (see page 14). Their houses were usually wooden with daub on the walls and thatch or reeds on the roof. In some parts of Britain the houses had stone walls and in north and west Scotland some people lived in *brochs*. These were very tall circular houses which protected them against attack.

Cutting the crop was done with an iron sickle. What is the modern equivalent? **Clue:** it is much larger!

Answer: Combine harvester

DYEING THEIR CLOTHES

Look at the front cover again. The Celtic warriors are wearing a variety of patterned clothes. To get these colours they dyed the yarn before weaving the material.

You can easily dye a piece of cloth yourself using natural dyes which the Celtic peoples had too. You will need to simmer the ingredients below in water with the material until you get the colour you want.

IF YOU WANT	USE
Brown	Birch bark
Yellow	The young shoots, flowers and bark of gorse
Black	Elder bark
Red-Orange	Dandelion root (in late summer) or the root of cleavers (goosegrass)
Blue	Various wild berries such as elderberries

There's another blue dye on page 13.

I spotted .... different wild plants to make different colour dyes on .... at ....

If you turn over you will see a drawing of a Celtic woman and man. Below is a picture of an *actual* Briton from the iron age, dating to about 300 BC. The body was uncovered by machines digging for peat in Lindow Moss, Cheshire in August 1984. Archaeologists nicknamed him Pete Marsh!

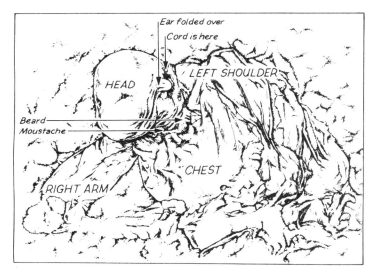

Lindow Man, as he became known, was found naked apart from a fox-fur band on his left arm. It is quite possible that he was naked when he died – Celtic warriors often fought naked – but the conditions in the marsh could have rotted away his clothes. He had been knocked unconscious with an axe and been struck in the back which broke one of his ribs. Then he was strangled with a cord which broke his neck. When he was dead, his throat was cut and he was dropped face down into a pool in the peat bog.

We know that the Celtic peoples thought that

Lindow Man

rivers and marshes were sacred and often threw finely-made objects there as offerings for the gods. We also know that they made sacrifices to the gods of animals *and* of human beings. Perhaps Lindow Man was a sacrifice to the gods. What do you think?

We have learnt something about the eating habits of the time from Lindow Man's stomach. The archaeological detectives found two sorts of wheat – spelt and emmer – and barley. There was also evidence of other plants which were probably growing in the cultivated cereal crop – Fat Hen, Dock, Meldes, Cow Parsley and Heather. Some of the bran and chaff of the cereals had been charred. It looked as if Lindow Man's last meal was bread – wholemeal type – which had been cooked, and partly burnt, on an open fire.

Extra **clue** to Lindow Man: his fingernails were carefully trimmed. What does that suggest?

Answer: He probably did not work with his hands or the fingernails would have been rough around the edges. Perhaps he was an important person in Celtic society.

Turn to page 16 for a recipe for Lindow Man's last meal.

Celtic art

The Celtic peoples loved finely made and decorated things such as mirrors, jewellery and weapons. The people who made them must have been very skilful.

Most of the decorated objects which survive from this period were made of metal – bronze, iron, gold and silver. Some of the decoration was *inscribed* – scratched – onto the surface of the object. Deeper lines were hammered on with a *punch*. You can see this sort of decoration on the mirror here – look for these basket-like lines.

Quite a lot of the decoration on Celtic objects is made up from regular patterns. Another great favourite was the horse. Here's one on a coin.

This is the decorated *back* of a bronze mirror. It was found at Desborough in Northamptonshire. The *front* is highly polished. Each half of the mirror has the same decoration. See if you can work it out and fill in the missing design. You may find it easier with compasses.

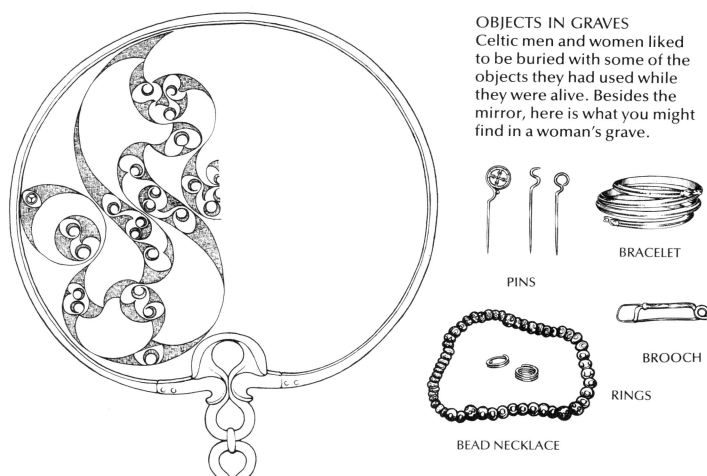

Have you hever seen a horse cut into the hillside like the one at Uffington in Oxfordshire?

OBJECTS IN GRAVES

Celtic men and women liked to be buried with some of the objects they had used while they were alive. Besides the mirror, here is what you might find in a woman's grave.

PINS

BRACELET

BROOCH

BEAD NECKLACE

RINGS

What would a man have been buried with?
Answer: Look on page 13

I saw Celtic jewellery at
....

Dress and fashion

Celtic women, and men, liked to wear jewellery. Some examples are pictured below and on the page opposite. See how many different examples you can find in museum collections. They wore rings — on their toes as well as on their fingers — bracelets and armbands, neckbands called *torques* and necklaces.

Sometimes the metal objects — jewellery and weapons — were inlaid with pink coral or red glass.

TORQUE

PENDANT

BROOCHES

They also wore different types of pins or brooches for fastening their clothes. Draw the modern equivalent of this one. **Clue:** babies usually have one of these.

She needs something to fasten her cloak
Don't forget the woad!
What's Missing?
Look at the range of patterns on the front cover

Complete and colour this drawing of a Celtic woman and man. You will find lots of clues to help you on this page and elsewhere in this book. Make up your own design for the man's shield.

Answer: safety pin

IN BATTLE

In battle, men sometimes wore helmets and carried shields. These were usually made of wood or leather but had metal parts too — the handle at the back and perhaps some decoration on the front. Some shields were faced entirely with decorated bronze and were probably only used for special ceremonies not for battle. To attack, they used swords and spears.

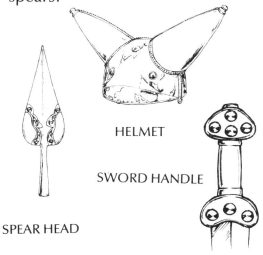

SPEAR HEAD

HELMET

SWORD HANDLE

BODY PAINT

We know that Celtic men liked to have their bodies decorated. Sometimes they were tattooed and sometimes painted with a blue dye from a plant called *woad*. They were fond of regular patterns like the ones on the mirror.

The Celts at war

One ancient writer said that the Celtic peoples were 'mad keen on war, full of spirit and quick to begin a fight'. They tried to make themselves look frightening and often washed their hair with lime and combed it to make it stand up on end like a porcupine's spikes. Naked to the waist, or sometimes completely naked, and painted with woad they rushed shouting into battle. The noise was increased by the animal-headed trumpet called a *carnyx*.

HILL FORTS

People started building defences on hill tops from about 1000BC. They were used as meeting places and for markets but were probably also religious or ritual centres. As the Celts became more warlike the defences of the hill forts became more and more impressive.

The drawing to the right shows one in Dorset today called Maiden Castle. It not only has a series of ditches and ramparts (walls of earth) but very complicated entrances. The distance from the top of the inner earth wall to the bottom of the ditch just in front was 14 metres!

 I visited a hill fort at

....

FIND THE CELTIC TRIBES

We know the names of the Celtic tribes in Britain because Roman writers and stone inscriptions recorded them. In the WORDSEARCH below you will find the names of 16 of the Celtic tribes which are listed on the map. One of those has already been ringed – look for the rest. By the way, they run diagonally, backwards, down and up!

O	S	E	T	A	B	E	R	T	A	B	I
P	A	R	I	S	I	J	L	O	E	N	T
D	U	M	N	O	N	I	I	L	U	E	R
Z	O	S	I	S	M	I	G	A	O	A	I
I	E	O	C	A	I	A	L	A	Q	V	N
I	P	T	E	C	E	L	N	K	V	O	O
V	I	U	N	N	E	T	U	B	E	G	V
O	D	A	I	V	I	M	N	R	M	L	A
N	I	B	U	I	A	D	G	L	E	E	N
R	I	T	A	E	Z	A	L	I	W	S	T
O	A	S	E	T	N	A	G	I	R	B	E
C	A	L	E	D	O	N	E	S	E	F	S

The front cover of this book shows a battle scene outside a hill fort like Maiden Castle.

Enter the Romans

The Romans invaded Britain in AD43 when Claudius was the Roman emperor. His 40,000 soldiers soon overcame even the fierce Celtic warriors. The Roman army gradually conquered the south of Britain although they had to fight many battles especially at hillforts like Maiden Castle. There was opposition to the Romans long after the invasion, especially from the Druids. The Romans hated the Druids because they stirred the people against them and because they did not like some of their religious practices such as human sacrifice.

THE DRUIDS' LAST STAND

In AD60, while Suetonius Paulinus was governor of Britain, there was a major revolt against Roman rule. Boudica queen of the Iceni tribe led a huge force against the Romans. After the killing of tens of thousands of Celtic people and Roman soldiers, she too was killed – the revolt was over.

Roman historians not only recorded important events like battles but also liked to add to the story by writing out speeches for commanders. We do not know, today, whether what the historian *said* the commanders said was true or not. Below is what the Roman historian Tacitus imagined the Roman commander and the British queen said to their troops.

Queen BOUDICA said:
'This is not the first time that we Britons have had women commanders in war. I am fighting as one of you for my freedom which the Romans have taken away. We have already massacred a Roman legion which dared to face us warlike Britons. Our gods will help us to victory today.'

Governor SUETONIUS PAULINUS said:
'Soldiers, take no notice of the noise and the yells of these savages – they have no discipline and there are more women than men in their army. You keep to your ranks, throw your javelins and rush forward to attack. Do not think of plunder now. Your victory today will give you all you need.'

You might like to colour in these figures.

Imagine a situation before the final battle when Boudica comes face to face with Suetonius Paulinus. What would you like them to say to each other? Put your ideas in the bubbles.

A CELTIC RECIPE

You might like to try making the sort of bread Lindow Man ate for his last meal. Buy some stone-ground/wholemeal wheat flour and mix it with barley flour (called bere flour) if you can get it in a wholefood shop. If you cannot buy it just use wholemeal flour.

Mix 100 grams of flour with 5 tablespoons of water until it makes a stiff paste. Form this dough into small flat rounds and under a very hot grill cook it for 2-3 minutes on each side. If you have a griddle or a heavy frying pan, try cooking the bread in a *little* fat by this method.

Lindow Man's bread would probably have been cooked in an open fire. If you try cooking on an open fire either use the griddle or take a sharpened stick, wrap the dough round the end and simply cook it in the flames.

If you want to discover more about prehistoric food a good book is *Food and Cooking in Prehistoric Britain* by Jane Renfrew published by English Heritage (1985).

LIVING IN THE IRON AGE

You can visit a reconstructed Celtic settlement complete with houses, crops and animals at Butser Ancient Farm in Queen Elizabeth Country Park, Gravel Hill, Horndean, near Petersfield, Hampshire.

FINDING OUT MORE

If you are interested in searching out more prehistory you might look out for:

Prehistory by Keith Branigan, published by Kingfisher Books (1984), looks at the prehistoric peoples in Europe.
Hunters and Early Farmers in Britain by Margaret Herdman, published by Harrap/Nelson (1982). This author has also written *Life in Iron Age Britain* (1981) in the same series.
The Penguin Guide to Prehistoric England and Wales by James Dyer (1981) is the best book you can get to help you find the best sites to visit.

Here are some good stories to read:
Blue Stones by Mary John, published by Barn Owl Press (1982), takes place at the time when Stonehenge was being built.
The Boy with the Bronze Axe by Kathleen Fidler, published by Penguin (1972), is about a boy who brings a bronze axe to people who were still using stone.
Sun Horse, Moon Horse by Rosemary Sutcliffe, published by Macmillan (1981), is set in the Celtic period.

The *Young Archaeologists Club* is a national club for children aged 9 and over. The club offers a variety of archaeological activities, a magazine four times a year and special holidays. If you would like more details write to Dr Kate Pretty, New Hall, Cambridge CB3 0DF.

English Heritage, which looks after nearly 400 of the most important monuments in England, has a special membership scheme for children called *Keep*. If you are interested, write for more information to English Heritage, PO Box 43, Ruislip, Middlesex HA4 0XW.

ANSWERS

Page 2: plastic and metal will survive best – camera, zips, wellingtons for example. Clothes will soon rot. Flesh rots quickly but hair and fingernails survive longer. Bones of the skeleton will probably last a very long time.

Page 4: did you fill in HORSE, REINDEER, BISON, RHINOCEROS and MAMMOTH correctly? They all survive today except the mammoth.

Page 6:   A   Bone shoulder blade from an ox used as a shovel
           B   Pick from a red deer's antler
           C   Axe of flint with a wooden handle

© 1986 The Trustees of the British Museum
Published by British Museum Publications
46 Bloomsbury Street, London WC1B 3QQ

ISBN 0-7141-1387-5

Typeset by Rowland Phototypesetting (London) Ltd
Printed in Great Britain by St Edmundsbury Press
Bury St Edmunds, Suffolk

Drawings by William Webb

The help and advice of members of staff of the Department of Prehistoric and Romano-British Antiquities in the British Museum is gratefully acknowledged.